Greater Than a Tourist Book Series
Reviews from Readers

I think the series is wonderful and beneficial for tourists to get information before visiting the city.

-Seckin Zumbul, Izmir Turkey

I am a world traveler who has read many trip guides but this one really made a difference for me. I would call it a heartfelt creation of a local guide expert instead of just a guide.

-Susy, Isla Holbox, Mexico

New to the area like me, this is a must have!

 -Joe, Bloomington, USA

This is a good series that gets down to it when looking for things to do at your destination without having to read a novel for just a few ideas.

-Rachel, Monterey, USA

Good information to have to plan my trip to this destination.

-Pennie Farrell, Mexico

Great ideas for a port day.

-Mary Martin USA

Aptly titled, you won't just be a tourist after reading this book. You'll be greater than a tourist!

-Alan Warner, Grand Rapids, USA

Even though I only have three days to spend in San Miguel in an upcoming visit, I will use the author's suggestions to guide some of my time there. An easy read - with chapters named to guide me in directions I want to go.

-Robert Catapano, USA

Great insights from a local perspective! Useful information and a very good value!

-Sarah, USA

This series provides an in-depth experience through the eyes of a local. Reading these series will help you to travel the city in with confidence and it'll make your journey a unique one.

-Andrew Teoh, Ipoh, Malaysia

GREATER THAN A TOURIST- SACRAMENTO CALIFORNIA USA

50 Travel Tips from a Local

Derek Steffen

Cover designed by: Ivana Stamenkovic
Cover Image: https://pixabay.com/photos/sacramento-california-city-1772563/

CZYK Publishing Since 2011.

Greater Than a Tourist

Lock Haven, PA
All rights reserved.

ISBN: 9781698263700

>TOURIST

50 TRAVEL TIPS FROM A LOCAL

BOOK DESCRIPTION

Are you excited about planning your next trip? Do you want to try something new? Would you like some guidance from a local? If you answered yes to any of these questions, then this Greater Than a Tourist book is for you. Most travel books tell you how to travel like a tourist. Although there is nothing wrong with that, as part of the Greater Than a Tourist series, this book will give you travel tips from someone who has lived at your next travel destination.

In these pages, you will discover advice that will help you throughout your stay. This book will not tell you exact addresses or store hours but instead will give you excitement and knowledge from a local that you may not find in other smaller print travel books.

Travel like a local. Slow down, stay in one place, and get to know the people and culture. By the time you finish this book, you will be eager and prepared to travel to your next destination.

Inside this travel guide book you will find:

- Insider tips from a local.

- Packing and planning list.

- List of travel questions to ask yourself or others while traveling.

- A place to write your travel bucket list.

OUR STORY

Traveling is a passion of the Greater than a Tourist book series creator. Lisa studied abroad in college, and for their honeymoon Lisa and her husband toured Europe. During her travels to Malta, an older man tried to give her some advice based on his own experience living on the island since he was a young boy. She was not sure if she should talk to the stranger but was interested in his advice. When traveling to some places she was wary to talk to locals because she was afraid that they weren't being genuine. Through her travels, Lisa learned how much locals had to share with tourists. Lisa created the Greater Than a Tourist book series to help connect people with locals. A topic that locals are very passionate about sharing.

TABLE OF CONTENTS

BOOK DESCRIPTION

OUR STORY

TABLE OF CONTENTS

DEDICATION

ABOUT THE AUTHOR

HOW TO USE THIS BOOK

FROM THE PUBLISHER

WELCOME TO

> TOURIST

1. What To Bring

2. Neighborhoods

3. Where To Stay

4. Stay Informed

5. Navigate the Airport

6. Get Around in a Car

7. Get Around Without a Car

8. Stay Safe

Places to Visit

9. Old Sacramento

10. Museums

11. State Parks

12. Regular Parks

13. Government

14. Support a Cause

15. Water

16. Libraries

17. For Kids

18. Nightlife

19. Untold History

Food & Drink

20. Farmer's Markets

21. Groceries

22. Festivals

23. Breakfast / Brunch

24. Lunch / Dinner

25. Dessert

26. Coffee

27. Breweries / Wineries

ART

28. Mural Walk

29. Second Saturdays

30. Movies

31. Music

32. Radio

SPORTS

33. Major Sports

34. Alternative Sports

35. Runs

SHOPPING

36. Shop Local

37. Glam Shopping

38. Vintage Shopping

SEASONAL

39. SacAnime

40. Car Shows

41. Tour of California

42. State Fair

43. Japanese Food & Culture Bazaar

44. Chalk It Up

45. The Day of the Dead

46. Christmas

SURROUNDING CITIES

47. To the North

48. To the East

49. To the West

50. To the South

TOP REASONS TO BOOK THIS TRIP:
OTHER RESOURCES:
TOP REASONS TO BOOK THIS TRIP
Packing and Planning Tips
Travel Questions
Travel Bucket List
NOTES

DEDICATION

This book is dedicated to Aidan and Cora, the future of Sacramento.

ABOUT THE AUTHOR

Derek is a father, husband, and Sacramento-based writer. He has lived and worked throughout the city his whole life. He and his wife are currently raising their two kids to appreciate and understand Sacramento the way they do.

HOW TO USE THIS BOOK

The *Greater Than a Tourist* book series was written by someone who has lived in an area for over three months. The goal of this book is to help travelers either dream or experience different locations by providing opinions from a local. The author has made suggestions based on their own experiences. Please check before traveling to the area in case the suggested places are unavailable.

Travel Advisories: As a first step in planning any trip abroad, check the Travel Advisories for your intended destination.
https://travel.state.gov/content/travel/en/traveladvisories/traveladvisories.html

FROM THE PUBLISHER

Traveling can be one of the most important parts of a person's life. The anticipation and memories that you have are some of the best. As a publisher of the Greater Than a Tourist, as well as the popular *50 Things to Know* book series, we strive to help you learn about new places, spark your imagination, and inspire you. Wherever you are and whatever you do I wish you safe, fun, and inspiring travel.

Lisa Rusczyk Ed. D.
CZYK Publishing

WELCOME TO
> TOURIST

"The real voyage of discovery consists not in seeking new landscapes but in having new eyes."

— Marcel Proust

Sacramento has long suffered from an identity crisis. Unsatisfied with its past reputation as a cow town, it dreams of being the next big American city. However, Sacramento slowly is realizing that you do not become great by being jealous of another's greatness.

Visiting Sacramento twenty years ago was a different experience than coming here today. Now the city has a better sense of who it is: a little bit of everything. Sacramento, as the above quote from Walt Whitman announces, is large and contains multitudes. Its traditions and its youth, its black and white history and its vibrant murals, its grand Capitol building and its tent shelters for the unhoused—these are not contradictions. This is the city.

Most who are born in Sacramento long to leave it for San Francisco, Los Angeles, or the East Coast. Sacramento is a place you must learn to love. Only over time do you come to cherish its diversity, respect its history, and treasure all it has to offer. I hope to speed that process up and give you fifty simple tips on how to get the most out of your visit to Sacramento.

Welcome!

BACKGROUND

Where you choose to stay in Sacramento and when you choose to visit will impact the experience you have. The further you stay away from the downtown area, the more time you will spend driving to get to where you want to be. Vacations should be for experiencing not commuting, so keep that in mind as you plan. Also, if you come here in the summertime, know that the heat is often around 100°F and may impact your enjoyment of the town. You can counter the warm weather with water, something to block out the sun, and positive vibes, but you should also plan on taking breaks and resting.

Sacramento
California, USA

1. WHAT TO BRING

If coming to Sacramento between May and September, expect heat. Sacramento's heat is a dry one but often flirts with triple-digit temperatures. As a result, you are going to want to make sure to have a hat and sunblock. The weather never gets too cold, but if you are arriving in the late fall or wintertime, a solid rain jacket goes a long way. The downtown area of Sacramento is walkable, so bring comfortable shoes. If you plan on visiting any of our parks, pack a picnic blanket. Very few businesses are cash only, so a credit card should suit you just about everywhere you go. You can also download Sacramento's parking app ahead of time to handle your parking needs.

2. NEIGHBORHOODS

Sacramento is a sprawling city comprised of distinct neighborhoods. Most traveling to the city for the first time will find themselves primarily in the downtown or midtown areas. Elsewhere, East Sacramento is a well-to-do sector of the city known for its expensive real estate. Times are tougher in South Sacramento, but you may want to sample its great ethnic cuisine options. West Sacramento is just across the Sacramento River, which acts as a border between the west area of town and what is generally referred to as downtown. Most of what you are going to want to see in West Sac is only a couple miles on the other side of the river boundary. The northern part of the city is primarily residential and, admittedly, will not entice even the most curious traveler.

3. WHERE TO STAY

As Sacramento covers a lot of territory, where are you choose to stay will impact how easily you can access what the city has to offer. There are smaller motels dotted throughout the city, but the most attractive accommodations are the larger hotels concentrated downtown. The most recent arrival is the Kimpton Sawyer, built in tandem with the city's new professional sports arena, the Golden 1 Center. The Sheraton Grand, the Citizen Hotel, and the Hyatt Regency are just a few more of the well-reviewed hotels located nearby. For a more novel stay, look into the Delta King, a docked riverboat in the historic Old Sacramento area. There are plenty of Airbnb options as well.

4. STAY INFORMED

Make the most of your visit by researching upcoming events ahead of time. For websites curated by people who live in the city, check out the Sacramento Downtown Grid and Sacramento Magazine. *The Sacramento Bee* and *Sacramento News and Review* are our publications of note if you are interested in reading about local current events. TV station KOVR has a regularly updated YouTube channel available for this same purpose. You may also want to follow #igerssac on Instagram for what residents are highlighting or peek around the Sacramento subreddit for what's on the minds of locals.

5. NAVIGATE THE AIRPORT

If you travel to Sacramento by plane, you will come through the Sacramento International Airport located just northwest of downtown Sacramento. The Sacramento International Airport is small and simple to navigate. However, if you are returning a rental automobile, know that all car rentals are held off-site. Factor in a shuttle ride from the return lot to the airport as a result. The airport's official webpage contains helpful information. You can track flights and also check how full the various parking lots are. Finally, depending on your arrival or departure time, you may experience increased traffic to or from the airport. This seldom has anything to do with the airport and is more a product of traffic on nearby Interstate-5. If accessing Sac International when people are going or coming from work, budget for more time.

6. GET AROUND IN A CAR

Sacramento drivers are unfortunately often ranked amongst the worst nationally. We have a reputation for being aggressive and inconsistent with our blinkers. In some parts of town, stop signs are looked at as more of an option than a mandate. In the downtown area, there are a plethora of one-way streets and a limited number of parking spots; subsequently, street parking can be tough. Calling a taxi or a rideshare company may be your best bet, or you can also rent a car through the GIG Share app.

7. GET AROUND WITHOUT A CAR

Once you have made it to town, depending on where you stay, a car is not entirely necessary. There are electric scooters and bikes for rent. Sacramento Regional Transit, the city's primary source of public transportation, provides buses and light rail options. Recently, they announced the addition of expanded services, including more late-night trips.

Overall, your best bet for getting from A to B could be your own two feet. Weather permitting, parts of Sacramento are definitely walkable, especially downtown and midtown. Twenty minutes of walking in July, however, is going to feel more taxing than twenty minutes in the early days of fall due to the heat. Plan accordingly.

8. STAY SAFE

To stay safe in Sacramento, apply common sense. Be mindful of your surroundings, and walk as a group if possible. Drivers rushing to beat traffic and streets with makeshift homeless camps are the only obstacles you will encounter. As long as you are smart and prepared, there should be no problems. If any violent crime does tend to happen in the touristy parts of town, it is seldom random and mostly occurs in the late nights of the weekend.

The emergency number in Sacramento is 911. To speak to the police in a non-emergency situation, call (916) 808-5471. For all other city-related issues, including broken parking meters, use 311.

PLACES TO VISIT

In Sacramento, what is interesting may not be obvious. Sacramento is not like a big city where the cool stuff is just going to jump out at you, but it is here, waiting. Challenge yourself to squeeze in a few atypical stops on your trip, some of which have been highlighted below. Also, know that there is an affordable version of a trip to Sacramento and an expensive one. None is the right choice, and both can be fulfilling. Unlike other major cities, you can get a lot out of Sacramento without paying a lot for it. Additionally, while Sacramento and the surrounding area are steeped in history, if history bores you, skip those suggested destinations. There are many different variations of a Sacramento vacation. Find the one that works best for you.

9. OLD SACRAMENTO

Buildings in Old Sacramento date back to the mid-1800s. Today, you can walk across its boardwalk and try out souvenir shops. Stage Nine is known for its memorabilia, while Evangeline's is the go-to spot for costumes and gag gifts. There are plenty of quirky eateries as well, like the presidential-themed Milk

House Shakes or the self-explanatory Danny's Mini Donuts.

Old Sacramento is nuzzled against the banks of the Sacramento River. You can take advantage of its location by strolling across the iconic Tower Bridge, stepping aboard the Delta King riverboat, or simply grabbing a seat on a bench overlooking the water. You may also want to reserve a spot on an underground tour, an hour-long guided walking trip around Old Sacramento that tells the story of its unique history and architecture. Additionally, there is a ghost tour available.

10. MUSEUMS

If you venture into Old Sacramento, there are many museums to try out. The most notable is the California State Railroad Museum. Here there are 21 locomotives and railroad cars on display, some of which you can walk through to get a sense of what travel was like two centuries ago. There is an excellent kids area on the top floor and also a screening room. During some parts of the year, you may even be able to ride upon a vintage locomotive for a scenic 45-minute trip along the Sacramento River.

If your appetite for historic travel is not satisfied by the railroad museum, hop on over to the California Automobile Museum. Throughout its 72,000 ft.^{2} of space, over 100 classic cars are on display with helpful docents ready to share their passion and knowledge with you.

If history, in general, is your thing, then stop by the California Museum. There are a few exhibits which are mainstays in the museum, but its revolving exhibitions are particularly exciting. Past displays have included Hollywood artifacts and cultural objects from the Hearst Castle.

All that being said, Sacramento's most prestigious museum is the Crocker Art Museum, the longest-running art museum in the western United States. Renovated in 2010, it celebrates past greatness and a bright future. Traditional styles and new artistic frontiers are given equal weight at the Crocker, as it offers a bit of everything. Additionally, thoughtful exhibits and creative programming, from youth art classes to film series and live performances, make the museum a must-see.

11. STATE PARKS

There are three primary state parks in Sacramento. The most recognizable, Sutter's Fort, is named after pioneer John Sutter. Chances are if you were ever a school child in town, you visited Sutter's Fort on a field trip. With 18-feet tall reinforced walls, the building was erected in the mid-1800s and served primarily as a center for agricultural production and trade. Despite its look and name, no battles were fought here, but it does make for a picturesque time machine to the past. After you get done exploring the fort, you can walk over to the Indian Museum or enjoy a picnic in front of a duck pond and fountain.

Another founding father of modern California was Leland Stanford. The Leland Stanford Mansion was recently given a multi-million dollar makeover and is now once more open to the public during regular business hours. This 19,000 ft.² residence was constructed in 1865. Its stately interiors are matched by its lovely gardens. Then, located a mile away, The Governor's Mansion is the last state park in Sacramento. While the current governor of California does not reside in the mansion, many in the past have. However, because it is not currently lived in, it does open for tours. Call ahead to make sure, because as governors change so too do vacancies and availability.

12. REGULAR PARKS

There are 222 parks in Sacramento. Depending on the time of year that you visit, a trip to the park can be the setting for a relaxing picnic. You can also use it as an opportunity for your kids to burn off energy.

Notable parks include Southside Park, just off of Broadway, with tennis and basketball courts, a pond for fishing, and two themed mid-sized playgrounds. William Land Park refers to one specific park, but locals tend to call the entire collection of green grassy areas nearby "Land Park." Land Park is in the heart of one of Sacramento's most established neighborhoods. Key features include a historic rock garden, a lily-filled duck pond with roaming geese, and multiple baseball fields. A tiny playground and numerous tables also make it a desired stop for weekend barbecues and birthday parties. Picture tip: Sunset, when the geese leave the park, makes for quite the image; conversely, you can get great photographs by snapping away at the lilies in the early morning.

Capitol Park is the name given to the outdoor public area surrounding the Capitol building. There are plenty of mature trees for shaded sitting, an Instagram-worthy rose garden, and several thoughtful memorials. Lastly, for a unique view of Sacramento, try the Emerald Tower Rooftop Park. Set atop an 18-story office building, you can get a bird's eye view of the city amongst beautifully curated landscapes (open to the public only during business hours).

City regulations require you to have pets on a leash in all public spaces, but you can toss a ball or throw a frisbee around at most locations. However, there are a few dog-only spaces in town, like Truitt Bark Park or Partner Park.

13. GOVERNMENT

As Sacramento is the centerpiece of California's state politics, government is a primary industry in town. This is evident in the many state office buildings that surround the Capitol and the Capitol itself. While you are here, why not check out democracy up-close? If the legislature is in session, you may be able to view bills being discussed and voted on from the public galleries that overlook the

Assembly and Senate floor. If you want to find a state representative more directly, there may also be opportunities to drop in on them in their offices.

In the basement of the Capitol, there is a museum with relics from the state's past. Tours are provided, and a trip to the gift shop should cap off any visit. County displays and stunning statues are located one level up on the first floor.

Even if you do not plan to go into the building, stop by for a memorable picture. The Capitol makes for quite the background. Its west side, along 10th Street, tends to be the most photographed. If there is a full moon during your stay, definitely try for a nighttime photoshoot.

14. SUPPORT A CAUSE

Sacramento is the seat of California's government, so there are political events or charitable gatherings happening regularly. The hub for this activity is the Capitol. On one day, you can participate in a fundraiser for the American Cancer Society. On another, you can rally in support of children's rights. Then there are protests against particular political issues you can join. If you are interested in taking part in any experiences like these, look into the Capitol's event calendar. This sort of direct action can be exciting to witness in person.

15. WATER

If traveling to Sacramento during warmer weather, you may be tempted to partake in either the American or Sacramento Rivers. The Sacramento River is predominantly known as a spot for boats and jet skis, and swimming is more common at the American. Sand Cove and Sutter's Landing are popular ports of entry to the river. Make sure to bring a life jacket and arrive early.

Just to the east, you can access Lake Natoma through the Sacramento State University Aquatic Center. This option is ideal for water sports, including kayaking and paddleboarding. For kids, there are splash pads and wading pools open in the summer, including Swanston Water Park and the Land Park Playground. If you want to get wet but in a more controlled environment, make time for Raging Waters theme park. Offering multiple slides and Northern California's first wave pool, Raging Waters has been in operation since 1980.

16. LIBRARIES

There are 28 library branches in the Sacramento public library system, making it the fourth largest in the state of California. If you want to beat the heat for a couple hours in the warmer months, libraries are a free and easy air-conditioned escape. Even without being a card-carrying patron, you can still access 3D printers, storytimes, and yoga classes. The Central Library is the largest branch in Sacramento. If you are near Central at sunset, when shadows fall on the many tall buildings downtown, the reflections in the glass windows are spectacular.

17. FOR KIDS

Kids will have plenty to do in Sacramento. If you are bringing little ones, you have to stop in the Land Park neighborhood and go to three Sacramento institutions: Funderland, the Sacramento Zoo, and Fairytale Town. Funderland offers a handful of understated amusement park rides. Fairytale Town is a story-book themed park with clean grounds and a variety of play areas. Then the Sacramento Zoo houses over 500 animals, including giraffes and orangutans. They are all within walking distance of each other. For older kids, other areas of interest in Sacramento may include our trampoline park (MojoDojo Extreme Sports), escape rooms (Enchambered Escape Rooms), and laser tag (Country Club Lanes).

18. NIGHTLIFE

The most frequented nightspots in Sacramento are found in the Lavender Heights section of town. This LGBTQ-focused area is welcoming to all (make sure to check out its rainbow crosswalk). The neighborhood's most notable club is Faces, which features three dance floors, fifteen bars, and a lax dress code.

Elsewhere, The Torch Club presents live blues music six days a week. If older music is your scene, consider LowBrau's Motown Mondays. Do you want to get in on the singing? Pine Cove Tavern hosts karaoke three times a week. If you are less musically inclined, then the Coin-Op Game Room might be what you are looking for. This pub showcases 40 classic arcade games and is open late for those 21 and older. Finally, the Sacramento Comedy Spot supports local comedians through its improv and open mic spotlights.

Currently, most bars and clubs close before 2 AM, although there is a push to extend hours until 4 AM. Regardless of their closing time, you will find the majority of these establishments to be most exciting Thursday through Saturday.

19. UNTOLD HISTORY

Much of what visitors tend to find special about Sacramento stems from all its history, persevered for generations in textbooks: the government, the Gold Rush, and more. However, there is a side of Sacramento not covered in school, a more infamous history that may be of interest to a particular kind of traveler. Be aware that the following trip suggestions are not for the easily disturbed.

Dorothea Puente ran a boarding house for the elderly. She preyed on her tenants by feeding them poison, burying them in her backyard, and then cashing their social security checks. The current owners of her old home at 2100 F Street have leaned into this ghastliness. T-shirts are sold, pictures encouraged, and tours held.

Another Sacramento menace was Richard Chase. From December 1977 to January 1978, Chase, known as the Vampire Killer of Sacramento, drank the blood of at least six victims. He lived at the Country Club Apartments on Watt Avenue.

Some believe that the old homes of Puente and Chase are now haunted. Other places in the area known to possess a troubled past and considered to be haunted include Dyer Lane, the Perrault House (5848 14th Avenue), and Seymour Park.

FOOD & DRINK

The range of what Sacramento has to offer food-wise is impressive. From its Michelin star restaurant The Kitchen to its food carts outside of churches, we have it all. There are far too many spots and types of food to include here. That being said, #sacfoodie is an instructive hashtag to follow. Also, if you find yourself staring at a menu and not sure what to order, ask a stranger around you or an employee—you tend to get reliable results this way.

20. FARMER'S MARKETS

Known as the Farm-to-Fork Capital, Sacramento features several farmer's market options. Buy fruits and vegetables straight from the farm, pick up a bouquet of lovely sunflowers, or eat local honey. Every Sunday of the year, you can browse local selections at 8th and W (under the freeway). Another all-year option is the Midtown Farmers Market, which is held every Saturday and tends to feature live music. May-to-September markets are also available, including those on Tuesdays at Roosevelt Park and Fremont Park, those on Wednesday at Cesar Chavez Park, and those on Thursdays along Capitol Mall.

21. GROCERIES

If you are looking to cook up some food while you are in town but want to shop from a store instead, Sacramento has most nationwide food chains. However, why not try something more regional? Smaller shops like Taylor's Market and Market 5-ONE-5 featured skilled butchers and organic produce. If you are interested in buying food and taking a cooking class, then Sacramento Natural Foods Co-op is for you. A laudable local chain is Nugget Markets. Nugget started in the mid-1920s, and today it touts many loyal customers who love its upscale shopping experience and variety of ready-made meals and baked goods

22. FESTIVALS

Where there is food, there are festivals. Sacramento is no different. The city offers year-round festivals for a variety of cuisines. Its most unique new offering is the Farm-to-Fork Festival. Since 2013, it has attracted 100,000 people per year and features vendors from throughout the state, chef preparations and demos, and even a dining club that eats upon the iconic Tower Bridge. The event is truly one of the premier music and food festivals in the country and generally family-friendly. Keep in mind that because the festival is hosted on Sacramento's Capitol Mall area, space and movement are at a minimum. At other times throughout the year, you can take part in a grilled cheese festival, a nacho festival, and even a bacon festival.

23. BREAKFAST / BRUNCH

If the breakfast options where you are staying are not satisfactory, allow Sacramento restaurants to provide you with that all-important first meal of the day. If you plan on arriving at these establishments after 9 AM on the weekend, prepare for a wait. Many do not take reservations over the phone, and parking can be difficult with everyone going out to eat at the same time. Plan ahead, consider sending a runner to save your place in line or sacrifice a little sleep to arrive early enough to get a table quickly.

Sacramento's most celebrated brunch institution is Tower Café in the shadow of the historic Tower Theater. You can choose to sit either in the outdoor garden area or amongst the eclectic design inside. Tower Café's menu is diverse with many options. In

East Sac, there's Orphan, which updates old classics with a Latin twist. Its coffee and tea menu is globally-inspired.

Another Sacramento favorite is downtown at Fox and Goose Public House. The original Fox and Goose Pub started in England centuries ago, but Sacramento's take on it began in the early 70s. The kitchen serves hearty pub food, and its atmosphere, from the history on the walls to the distinctive early-1900s brick architectural design, adds to the experience. If you want a more tucked away breakfast downtown, Wild Flour Cafe is a newer spot in a mostly residential area. Wild Flour's menu highlights locally sourced salads, baked goods, and house-made sausages. All four of these options are going to run you about $10-$25 per person, depending on what beverages are ordered.

If you want a more inexpensive experience, you can head out to the Stagecoach Restaurant in South Sac and enjoy country-style comfort food amongst unique stagecoach decor. From their country-fried steak to their braised oxtail, their menu can leave you feeling a little heavy. Partake in a bit of light exercise afterward. Lastly, If you consider yourself a pancake connoisseur, then you must make time for Harry's Cafe. Harry's pancakes do not feature any bells or whistles—just basic pancakes down exceptionally well. In addition to American classics, they also spotlight Vietnamese and Chinese breakfast options.

24. LUNCH / DINNER

Sacramento is known for being one of the most ethnically diverse cities in the country. You can find just about every different type of food here. Some neighborhoods tend to feature one type of cuisine more than any other. As an example, the best Mexican food you are going to find will be in South Sacramento, for instance, at Lalo's Restaurant. In the same part of Sacramento, there are also many strong Chinese options, including Sunrise Chinese Restaurant. Both feature quality food at an affordable price point.

For Thai food, there are several options on Broadway, like Chada Thai, which is down the street from an Ethiopian staple, Queen Sheba, and not too far from several ramen-centric restaurants, for example, Ryujin.

Sacramento also has bistro-style restaurants galore. The sandwiches at 33rd Street Bistro are sure to impress. If you like the atmosphere of a tavern, then stop by Pangaea Bier Cafe. Their special sauce has helped their burger win local burger battles multiple years in a row. If fried chicken and smoked meats are what you crave, then prime all your senses for the selections at South. If you just want to grab a slice of pizza, then make sure to stop by Uncle Vito's, where they have generous sizes and the best crust in town.

As you can tell, there are many great sit-down options in Sacramento. As far as fast food, you may want to consider Jimboy's, a local quick-service stop serving up simple Mexican meals since the 1950s. While delicious, their tacos require an extra napkin or two. Also, do not forget Sacramento's burgeoning food truck scene. Food trucks typically hang out in the downtown area during the workday and frequent festivals at night. For specific truck locations, look into social media accounts. As far as particular trucks, if you are in the mood for Nashville style chicken, there's Nash and Proper. For freshly made tortillas, Masa Guiseria is a must.

25. DESSERT

If you want to indulge your sweet tooth, there are several other Sacramento staples to know about. Local landmarks like Vic's in the Land Park neighborhood or Gunther's in the Curtis Park area constantly battle for who has the best ice cream in town. Try a flavor you have never had before, like raspberry ribbon or pumpkin, and enjoy a cone either under the neon glow of Gunther's or amongst the old-school stylings of Vic's. For a refreshing treat of a different variety, there is shaved ice at Osaka-Ya. Osaka-Ya is a cash-only business open during warm months. Their sizes are quite substantial, so a small should satisfy most appetites. Another seasonal favorite is the peach milkshakes at Whitey's Jolly Kone just across the river in West Sacramento.

The best cookies in town are at Ginger Elizabeth Chocolates. The fruit pies at the Real Pie Company are delicious and baked in-store. Rick's Dessert Diner is known for its classic look and mouth-watering cakes. If you are going to be in town with a group for a while, consider a custom order at Freeport Bakery (a Ken Doll cake of theirs went viral in 2016).

Beyond baked goods, Andy's Candy Apothecary, a thoughtfully curated downtown candy store, should do the trick. Finally, whether morning or night, Marie's Donuts is always the right choice.

26. COFFEE

In Sacramento, you do not have to settle for national coffee chains. We certainly have those, but there are many local options as well. Old Soul serves up Ethiopian beans. Temple will delight you with its Guatemala Hunapu Antigua Bourbon coffee. Chocolate Fish makes mochas as fabulous to look at as they are to drink, while Identity will turn you on to the balanced flavor of a cortado. When you come to a new city, you should try a new experience. This goes for your coffee too.

27. BREWERIES / WINERIES

You must be 21 or older to drink alcohol in California, but if you are, we have a wide selection to choose from. For beer-first folks, there are over fifty local breweries. Pay close attention to which breweries source their ingredients locally.

Full of hops, the Panic IPA at Track 7 is a favorite. Device serves a chocolate-infused stout called Brits in Moscow. New Glory has on tap a milkshake IPA with a pineapple taste appropriately named the Mindshaker. Then if you prefer your beer with exercise thrown into the mix, you can reserve a 15-

person Brew Bike for a guided tour of the local craft beer scene.

If wine is more your fancy, we also have you covered. The Underground Tasting Room features a friendly environment and award-winning wines direct from regional wineries, while Revolution Wines crushes and ferments their grapes on-site.

Sacramento
Climate

	High	Low
January	56	41
February	62	44
March	68	47
April	74	49
May	82	54
June	89	59
July	94	61
August	93	61
September	89	59
October	79	53
November	65	46
December	56	41

GreaterThanaTourist.com

Temperatures are in Fahrenheit degrees.
Source: NOAA

ART

Sacramento has pushed to rebrand itself as a haven for visual artists. From the ever-growing Crocker Art Museum to the Oscar-nominated, Sacramento-set film *Lady Bird*, the city has grown tremendously in this regard over the last decade. In particular, you will see many public spaces used to showcase art. If searching for eye-catching shots to feature on your Instagram, Sacramento has just what you need.

28. MURAL WALK

Wayne Thiebaud remains Sacramento's most celebrated visual artist, but the city has recently tried to foster a reputation as being a hotspot for art. The most prominent way this has been done is through Wide Open Walls. Since 2016, every August, world-renowned muralists descend on the walls of the city to leave their color and creativity behind. Shepard Fairey's towering tribute to Johnny Cash and a recycled-goods depiction of an orangutan family are a few of the highlights. To view all these pieces is free and many are within walking distance of each other. A map is available online.

A similar endeavor, though on a much smaller scale, is the Capital Box Art project. Several years ago, a local property management group began transforming traffic utility boxes into canvases worthy of a museum. These boxes have been wrapped with creations from local artists and are waiting for you to strap on your walking shoes, pull up the online map, and see them all.

29. SECOND SATURDAYS

Once a month, hundreds descend on a handful of midtown blocks to partake in a nighttime art walk. In theory, the event is to look at, appreciate, and even buy art, but the focus tends to be more on enjoying the social atmosphere. If attending, plan on walking from stop to stop. Most people just mill around the entire evening, partaking in live music or enjoying an adult beverage. Also, be prepared to park your car a bit away from the center of action.

30. MOVIES

When on a trip, seeing a movie is not usually on the schedule. However, Sacramento is home to a few unique cinematic experiences you may not want to miss. While most cities nowadays, including Sacramento, have theaters with recliners and alcoholic beverages flowing, we have a few alternatives as well. For instance, you can see a film festival at the Crest Theater, which first opened in 1912. Then there's the Tower Theatre, which was built in 1938. Its marquee is one of the most photographed objects in the whole city. Any traveling cinephile should also appreciate the grand scale of the Esquire IMAX Theatre or the throwback appeal of the West Wind Drive-In (Tuesdays are discount days).

31. MUSIC

Music often plays alongside of Sacramento's many festivals and outdoor events. If you are in town and want to see a formal show, top local venues include Ace of Spades, the Golden 1 Center, and B St Theater. As with most places downtown, when you are headed towards a large gathering, especially on a weekday, give yourself extra time before the show to find parking.

For the indie music fan, there is the City of Trees multi-day festival in September. September is also home to the Aftershock Festival, which features big names in rock.

For free music, if you are here in the summer, Curtis Park hosts a monthly Music in the Park concert series, while East Sac hosts Pops in the Park. Both are no-charge family-oriented events. Sacramento State University also typically offers free student recitals. This is an excellent opportunity to see blossoming local talent in a formal musical setting.

32. RADIO

If you are driving in a new city, you may find it helpful to know what local radio stations are playing. 102.5 KSFM features R&B, Hip-Hop, and Rhythmic Pop. Top 40 lives at 106.5 The End. Alt 94.7 plays a mix of 90s songs and hitmakers from the modern indie scene. 105.1 KNCI is Sacramento's home for country music. 98 Rock (98.5) serves up mainstream rock, but if you are into the classics, like Led Zeppelin and Aerosmith, tune into 96.9 The Eagle. If you have a good antenna and are more adventurous, dial over to 90.3 KDVS. KDVS is a college station broadcasting from nearby Davis that showcases a variety of genres and artists you may have never heard of. Finally, if you want FM talk radio, try 90.9, Capital Public Radio, for local programming and NPR shows.

SPORTS

A turning point in the development of the downtown Sacramento area came when the Sacramento Kings broke ground on their new arena, the Golden 1 Center, in 2014. Sacramento residents have not always had much to cling to other than professional basketball. Fittingly, as the city grows in national prominence, the Kings have moved downtown to the center stage of Sacramento.

33. MAJOR SPORTS

Sacramento has three major sports teams. The Sacramento Kings basketball team is the longest-running of the three. The beautiful new Golden 1 Center downtown was built to host their games, and the current iteration of the team plays a quick and exciting brand of basketball. There are food options inside the arena that are just as enticing as the on-court action.

Second oldest is the Sacramento River Cats, a minor league baseball affiliate of the San Francisco Giants. Games are played in West Sacramento (Sutter Health Park). If you are coming with little ones and looking for cheaper seats, you can buy tickets to sit out on the grass along the third-base side or behind right field. Bring a picnic blanket.

Finally, there's the Sacramento Republic Football Club. Part of the USL Championship league, Sac Republic has a passionate fanbase that comes out loudly for every soccer match. The city has plans to erect a new arena, but for now, the team plays on the grounds of Cal Expo at Papa Murphy's Park.

34. ALTERNATIVE SPORTS

If you are interested in watching local sports but not at the professional level, Sacramento has a variety of choices for you as well. Sacramento Roller Derby is a fast-moving sport to fire up the whole family. There are different levels of tickets, and those in the VIP range come with food.

High-profile professional wrestling comes to the Golden 1 Center several times per year, but for local independent talent, there's the Total Wrestling

Federation. These gritty wrestlers perform throughout town with a Christmas show every year at the Colonial Theatre.

Track and field aficionados will want to see if any meets are coming up at Sacramento State University. In the past, Sacramento has hosted both Olympic qualifying and Junior Olympics tournaments. Lastly, if you do not want to be a mere spectator, there are bowling, golf, and mini-golf options. Capital Bowl has renovated lanes and a stellar kitchen. Bing Maloney has a driving range and a Champion 18 hole course, while Scandia Family Fun Center has two Scandanavian-themed putt-putt courses. For both golf options, try not to play between 1-6 PM during the summertime to avoid overheating.

35. RUNS

Come to stay in shape or use a race as an excuse to visit Sacramento. You can typically find at least one event per weekend. The Color Run is a fun 5k that will leave you covered from head to toe in colored powder. The Run to Feed the Hungry (5k/10k) is the largest Thanksgiving run in the United States. The Urban Cow Half Marathon leans into Sacramento's cowtown reputation, and you will find more than a few cowbells amongst the runners that come out every October. If a half marathon does not satisfy, then go for the whole 26.2 miles at the California International Marathon. This race, which has seen national records set, starts in the nearby town of Folsom before finishing at the State Capitol.

SHOPPING

Local business owners are invested in their shops and communities. As a result, you should receive a more curated shopping experience and more attentive customer service at these businesses than you would receive at a national chain store. In this way, responsible travel supports the local economy, but it also benefits you, the traveler.

36. SHOP LOCAL

If you do plan on making any kind of purchase in Sacramento, always try to think locally. Yes, there are many big-name chains here, but you can find those everywhere; instead, you should support local businesses with your wallet. In this way, as you take something from the city, you will also be giving something back. We have many Sacramento-only hobby and gift shops throughout town.

You can satisfy your fairy needs at The Secret Garden. Into miniatures? Then you have to go to Elegant Dollhouse. Used and new books can be found at Beers Books. Make your purchase sassy at Mixed Bag. Buy guilt-free handcrafted imported jewelry at Zanzibar Trading Co. or grab a quirky bowtie at Strapping Store.

If you happen to be here around the Christmas holiday, you can also find numerous craft fairs. In many cases, you will be buying directly from the makers of your items, which adds a whole other level of awesome to the concept of shopping locally.

37. GLAM SHOPPING

If you want to shop at high-end, name-recognizable stores, you are going to have to venture outside of the city center. For instance, there is a Tiffany's at the Roseville Galleria about twenty-five minutes outside of Sacramento and a Kate Spade at the Folsom outlets about as far away as well. Closer in town, along Fair Oaks Boulevard, is Pavillions, a sophisticated shopping center offering many high-quality men's and women's apparel options. If you want younger, trendier stores, you are better off going to midtown, specifically R Street and the Ice Blocks development, or around the Golden 1 Center.

Other fashion boutiques can be found throughout downtown, including the super cute Wild Poppy and the ethically-conscious Purpose. If you are more in the mood for streetwear selections, Getta Clue has been a mainstay of the Sacramento scene since 1992.

38. VINTAGE SHOPPING

Want to come back with a stellar outfit but at a lower price? Sacramento has many secondhand, thrift, or vintage clothing options. There are national non-profits like Goodwill and the SPCA Adoptable Goods store, but you should also look into TRUE. TRUE's proceeds go to support intervention services for local survivors of domestic and sexual abuse. Then there is Thrift Town, which was featured in the 2017 award-winning movie *Lady Bird*. Finally, Ed's Threads caters to dapper men searching for old school style.

SEASONAL

The majority of the events highlighted below only come around once per year, and locals look forward to them just as much as you may when planning your trip. As a result, try to get to these events as close to their starting time as possible. Always add an extra ten minutes because of parking.

39. SACANIME

If you are into pop culture with a manga and anime focus, you will want to attend SacAnime. Hosted semi-annually (January and June), this festival, which draws about 15,000, is situated throughout Sacramento, though increasingly is headquartered at Cal Expo. Cosplay, KPOP battles, and art contests are sure to thrill, while you may be lucky enough to snag an autograph from a professional voice actor or artist. If you want to wave your geek flag even more proudly, do some tabletop gaming at Great Escape Games or grab a beverage and reading material at Oblivion Comics & Coffee (cosplay encouraged but no masks allowed).

40. CAR SHOWS

If you were in Sacramento in the 90s, then you knew Sundays as cruising days. Every weekend beautiful hot rods and lowriders would travel slowly up and down Broadway. Law enforcement eventually broke these meetings up, but their spirit lives on in the city's car culture. You can see these rides in action at various events throughout the year, most notably at Back to the Boulevard (Franklin Boulevard) every September or the Cruise Fest, sponsored by the California Automobile Museum, every October. However, Sacramento's longest-running ode to cars started seventy years ago with the Sacramento Autorama. The Autorama is the oldest indoor car show in the world. For three days every February, thousands descend on Cal Expo to take in hundreds of classic, custom, and futuristic cars.

41. TOUR OF CALIFORNIA

Officially "The Amgen Tour of California," every May since 2006, a 773-mile bike race comes through Sacramento. Sacramento is the site of Stage 1 of this seven-day internationally-recognized tournament. This first stage is an 88-mile sprint that takes riders across the iconic Tower Bridge before finishing in front of the State Capitol. On this day, you will find many streets closed off. As Sacramento already has construction detours in constant rotation, driving around the city during events is especially tricky, particularly for newbies. Be patient. You can typically ask police officers positioned at detour sites for the best approach to driving to where you need to be. Again, non-car travel is encouraged in the downtown area at all times, particularly when events are taking place. By the way, May is fittingly Sacramento's bike month, so you can act like a local and grab something with two wheels. Electric JUMP bikes are located throughout town and accessed through a mobile app, while Practical Cycles has a variety of bike styles to rent as you explore the city.

42. STATE FAIR

One of Sacramento's premier events is the California State Fair. Held every July, it features all manner of rides, performances, and food. Like most prominent events in the area, the fair is located at Cal Expo, where you will pay to park, pay to get in, and then still need to pay for rides and meals. The good

July 4
-30

55

news is that Tuesdays are discount days, and you can easily spend all day here. If you do end up spending a large chunk of time at the fair, you are going to want to be mindful about when you are outside. Sacramento gets so hot during the summer that too much sun will zap you of your energy. While you can bring in sealed water bottles to the fair, it is also recommended that you arrive early. Do as much as you can outside first, like attractions and livestock, and then head to the indoor, air-conditioned county exhibits and demos.

As far as food, healthy options are at a minimum, so go ahead and indulge in some fabulous funnel cake. Please note that while every guest must enter through metal directors, each year there is at least one night that is marred by a fistfight. However, these fights tend to be between teenaged guests and isolated to late at night on the weekends.

43. JAPANESE FOOD & CULTURE BAZAAR

The Japanese and Japanese-Americans in Sacramento have a complicated history due to their forced internment during World War II. Relatedly, the Japanese Food & Culture Bazaar is a two-day festival held every August that has been going for over seventy years. The event started after the Japanese-Americans in the area began rebuilding their lives following their forced relocation.

25,000 people attend annually. Cultural performances are featured, including Taiko drumming. You can also view Japanese calligraphy and flower arrangements (*ikebana*). The star of the weekend, however, is all the available food. Hundreds of pounds of shrimp are prepared for shrimp tempura each year, while thousands of pounds of chicken are readied for chicken teriyaki. The event is held at the Buddhist Church of Sacramento, and all parking must be done off-site. A courtesy shuttle is provided from a nearby city lot.

44. CHALK IT UP

Every Labor Day weekend, Fremont Park, in the heart of midtown, is host to a three-day art extravaganza known as Chalk It Up. Chalk It Up is a non-profit arts event going into its third decade. Participants are personally sponsored or sponsored by local businesses to create chalk masterpieces in the concrete squares along the park. At times throughout the weekend, things get tight, because the artists need to use the walkway to create and the immediate space around each square for their supplies and themselves. Throw in some vendors and food trucks, and it turns quickly into a crowded though memorable weekend. Kids can play in the park's gated playground. If you do not want to go when it is packed but still want to see the finished work, aim to be there early Labor Day evening or shortly after. Footprints tend to have obscured most of the art a day or two after the event.

45. THE DAY OF THE DEAD

Día de los Muertos (The Day of the Dead) is a multi-day celebration beginning on the last day of October. The Day of the Dead comes from Mexico and recognizes family members who have passed on. The holiday is most closely associated with sugar skulls and the Pixar movie *Coco*. Sacramento is heavily influenced by its Mexican and Mexican-American population, so the Day of the Dead is a big deal here. Throughout the city, you will find many exhibits, art opportunities, and music. Community celebrations revolve around shared food and often take place inside cemeteries. The art-based organization Sol Collective is a driving force behind Day of the Dead happenings. Another important event for those in the area with Mexican heritage is Día de la Virgen de Guadalupe (The Day of the Virgin of Guadalupe). On this day, Catholics throughout the region honor the Blessed Virgin Mary. This is especially so at the Our Lady of Guadalupe Church across from Southside Park. Many vendors are present.

46. CHRISTMAS

Christmas in Sacramento is a magical time. While we do not get snow like our neighbors to the north, there are enough holiday activities to cure any curmudgeon. The season begins with the Theatre of Lights, a free multimedia show held in Old Sacramento that pits Santa Claus against Jack Frost. Shows start the day after Thanksgiving. Right across the way, you can purchase tickets for a ride on the railroad museum's Polar Express. Tickets go fast, so be ready to pounce on them as soon as they are available online. Even if you are unable to get tickets, you can still stop by to see the beautifully themed decorations outside the train's entryway. Old Sacramento is also home to the Sacramento Lighted Boat Parade every December.

Speaking of Christmas lights, you have to stop by the Fab 40s in East Sac. The Fab 40s is the name given to a series of blocks in ritzy East Sac, where each year million-dollar homes are decorated to the nth degree. Many people park and then get out to walk up and down the streets. Caroling is encouraged.

Back downtown, you can skate at the city's outdoor ice rink, take in the annual Santa parade, and watch the giant Christmas tree lighting outside the State Capitol. While you are at the Capitol, look into the Capitol Holiday Music Program. Local choirs fill the building with their holiday cheer for multiple performances in November and December.

SURROUNDING CITIES

One of the remarkable things about Sacramento is its proximity to other great travel destinations. Within a mere two hour drive, for example, you can change your environment completely. Sacramento is a fantastic starting place for a day trip out of town. The tips below highlight destinations all within about an hour's car trip from the city center. Where you stay when you are in town or what time you choose to head out can impact how long it takes to get to where you are going. Leaving Sacramento in the morning on a weekday does not usually present too much traffic, but it certainly will on the weekend. (The opposite is true: if you are coming into town in the morning on a weekday, expect traffic, as most people commute downtown for work.)

47. TO THE NORTH

If you head two hours north of Sacramento, you end up in Lake Tahoe, which is world-famous for all of its natural beauty. There are, however, destinations before that point that may be worth a day trip of your time. Twenty-five minutes outside of Sacramento lies the city of Rocklin. Rocklin is home to the newly-built Quarry Park, an outdoor adventure park with ziplines, rock climbing, and rappel walls. The park is open most of the week from the early morning until late evening, and there is easily a day's worth of activities here. Also, twenty-five minutes outside of Sacramento is the city of Roseville. In Roseville, you can skydive indoors at iFLY, go shopping at Coach or Burberry at the Galleria, or call back the past at the Roseville Telephone Museum. Further down the road, about forty-five minutes from Sacramento, the town of Auburn offers serene Lake Clementine. The lake is a 3.5-mile gem available for water-skiing, kayaking, and fishing. You can also hike or bike the nearby trail, which leads to a stunning waterfall.

48. TO THE EAST

If you head several hours east of Sacramento, you end up in Yosemite, a national park located against the Sierra Nevada mountain range. There are, however, destinations before that point that may be worth a day trip of your time. Approximately thirty minutes outside of the city is Folsom. Here you can take in a show at the Harris Center, visit the Folsom State Prison Museum, or wander amongst free-roaming peacocks at the Folsom City Zoo Sanctuary. Further east, the city of Placerville is fifty minutes away. In Placerville lies Apple Hill, which is worthy of a visit most of the year but especially in the fall. Any kind of delicious apple beverage or food you can think of is sold here. You can tour local orchards and pick out the freshest apples or spend an afternoon sampling wine amongst the natural splendor of the area. This is a great destination for families or adults on their own. Finally, clocking in at just under an hour's drive from Sacramento, the city of Jackson is one more potential stop in an eastern direction. Your best options are to dive into Gold Rush history at the Kennedy Gold Mine or to try to strike it rich at Jackson Rancheria casino. The casino features over

1,700 slot machines and a variety of gaming tables. You must be 18 years of age or older to gamble.

49. TO THE WEST

If you head several hours west of Sacramento, you end up in prime wine country. There are, however, destinations before that point that may be worth a day trip of your time. Davis is twenty minutes away and home to the University of California Davis. At the university, you can visit its majestic public gardens, browse its unique botanical conservatory, and explore the pristine Manetti Shrem Museum for Art. Then thirty minutes to the west of Sacramento is Vacaville, where you will find The Nut Tree, which was built in 1921. Today it is home to a family-friendly play area, an adjacent small airport, and many retail stores and restaurants, like Fentons Creamery. Fentons serves up some of the best ice cream you will ever have. If the small scale amusement offerings of Sacramento or Vacaville do not satisfy, head fifty minutes west to Vallejo's Six Flags Discovery Kingdom. From thrill rides to kid rides, animal encounters to fright shows, Six Flags is one of the top theme parks in all of California.

50. TO THE SOUTH

Heading six hours south of Sacramento, you end up in the Los Angeles area. There are, however, destinations before that point that may be worth a day trip of your time. A one-time suburb of Sacramento but now its own city, Elk Grove is fifteen minutes away. If you are around for Christmas and have already exhausted the holiday activities listed above, then check out its Dickens Street Faire. Carolers, costumed entertainers, and a special appearance by Santa transport you to a magical, simpler time. Next, you can head twenty minutes outside Sacramento to Clarksburg and the Old Sugar Mill. Here there are a dozen wineries and a gorgeous grass area perfect for picnicking. Lastly, for a one-of-kind experience, try Locke, a historic Chinese community built over 100 years ago and only thirty minutes away from Sacramento. Locke is so small you can drive through it in less than sixty seconds, but it is full of history and great spots to photograph.

TOP REASONS TO BOOK THIS TRIP:

History: In and around Sacramento, you can celebrate the old in exciting new ways.

Food: In Sacramento, you can sample a diverse offering of cultural cuisines.

Art: In Sacramento, you can witness beauty on walls, in museums, and at local galleries and shops.

Ease of Access: In Sacramento, getting around has never been easier, so plan your visit today.

OTHER RESOURCES:

City of Sacramento Parking:
http://www.cityofsacramento.org/public-works/parking-
services/street-parking/parkmobile

City of Sacramento Maps:
https://www.cityofsacramento.org/ParksandRec/Neighbor
hood-Services/Maps

Tracking Airport Flights and Parking:
https://sacramento.aero/smf

Events at the Capitol:
https://capitolpermits.chp.ca.gov/Event/EventCalendar

Mural Walk (Wide Open Walls):
https://www.wideopenwalls.com/map/

Capitol Box Art:
http://capitolboxart.com/map/

PACKING AND PLANNING TIPS

A Week before Leaving

- Arrange for someone to take care of pets and water plants.

- Email and Print important Documents.

- Get Visa and vaccines if needed.

- Check for travel warnings.

- Stop mail and newspaper.

- Notify Credit Card companies where you are going.

- Passports and photo identification is up to date.

- Pay bills.

- Copy important items and download travel Apps.

- Start collecting small bills for tips.

- Have post office hold mail while you are away.

- Check weather for the week.

- Car inspected, oil is changed, and tires have the correct pressure.

- Check airline luggage restrictions.

- Download Apps needed for your trip.

Right Before Leaving

- Contact bank and credit cards to tell them your location.

- Clean out refrigerator.

- Empty garbage cans.

- Lock windows.

- Make sure you have the proper identification with you.

- Bring cash for tips.

- Remember travel documents.

- Lock door behind you.

- Remember wallet.

- Unplug items in house and pack chargers.

- Change your thermostat settings.

- Charge electronics, and prepare camera memory cards.

READ OTHER
GREATER THAN A TOURIST
BOOKS

Greater Than a Tourist- Geneva Switzerland: 50 Travel Tips from a Local by Amalia Kartika

Greater Than a Tourist- St. Croix US Birgin Islands USA: 50 Travel Tips from a Local by Tracy Birdsall

Greater Than a Tourist- San Juan Puerto Rico: 50 Travel Tips from a Local by Melissa Tait

Greater Than a Tourist – Lake George Area New York USA: 50 Travel Tips from a Local by Janine Hirschklau

Greater Than a Tourist – Monterey California United States: 50 Travel Tips from a Local by Katie Begley

Greater Than a Tourist – Chanai Crete Greece: 50 Travel Tips from a Local by Dimitra Papagrigoraki

Greater Than a Tourist – The Garden Route Western Cape Province South Africa: 50 Travel Tips from a Local by Li-Anne McGregor van Aardt

Greater Than a Tourist – Sevilla Andalusia Spain: 50 Travel Tips from a Local by Gabi Gazon

Children's Book: *Charlie the Cavalier Travels the World* by Lisa Ruszczyk

> TOURIST

Follow us on Instagram for beautiful travel images:
http://Instagram.com/GreaterThanATourist

Follow *Greater Than a Tourist* on Amazon.
>Tourist Podcast
>T Website
>T Youtube
>T Facebook
>T TikTok
>T Goodreads
>T Amazon
>T Mailing List
>T Pinterest
>T Instagram
>T Twitter
>T SoundCloud
>T LinkedIn
>T Map

> TOURIST

At *Greater Than a Tourist*, we love to share travel tips with you. How did we do? What guidance do you have for how we can give you better advice for your next trip? Please send your feedback to GreaterThanaTourist@gmail.com as we continue to improve the series. We appreciate your constructive feedback. Thank you.

METRIC CONVERSIONS

TEMPERATURE

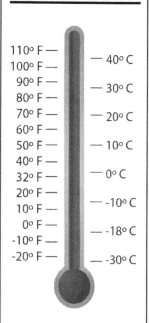

110° F	
100° F	— 40° C
90° F	
80° F	— 30° C
70° F	
60° F	— 20° C
50° F	— 10° C
40° F	
32° F	— 0° C
20° F	
10° F	— -10° C
0° F	— -18° C
-10° F	
-20° F	— -30° C

To convert F to C:

Subtract 32, and then multiply by 5/9 or .5555.

To Convert C to F:

Multiply by 1.8 and then add 32.

32F = 0C

LIQUID VOLUME

To Convert:...................Multiply by
U.S. Gallons to Liters................ 3.8
U.S. Liters to Gallons 26
Imperial Gallons to U.S. Gallons 1.2
Imperial Gallons to Liters....... 4.55
Liters to Imperial Gallons 22
1 Liter = .26 U.S. Gallon
1 U.S. Gallon = 3.8 Liters

DISTANCE

To convert ....Multiply by
Inches to Centimeters 2.54
Centimeters to Inches 39
Feet to Meters...................... .3
Meters to Feet 3.28
Yards to Meters 91
Meters to Yards 1.09
Miles to Kilometers 1.61
Kilometers to Miles............ .62
1 Mile = 1.6 km
1 km = .62 Miles

WEIGHT

1 Ounce = .28 Grams
1 Pound = .4555 Kilograms
1 Gram = .04 Ounce
1 Kilogram = 2.2 Pounds

TRAVEL QUESTIONS

- Do you bring presents home to family or friends after a vacation?

- Do you get motion sick?

- Do you have a favorite billboard?

- Do you know what to do if there is a flat tire?

- Do you like a sun roof open?

- Do you like to eat in the car?

- Do you like to wear sun glasses in the car?

- Do you like toppings on your ice cream?

- Do you use public bathrooms?

- Did you bring your cell phone and does it have power?

- Do you have a form of identification with you?

- Have you ever been pulled over by a cop?

- Have you ever given money to a stranger on a road trip?

- Have you ever taken a road trip with animals?

- Have you ever went on a vacation alone?

- Have you ever run out of gas?

- If you could move to any place in the world, where would it be?

- If you could travel anywhere in the world, where would you travel?

- If you could travel in any vehicle, which one would it be?

- If you had three things to wish for from a magic genie, what would they be?

- If you have a driver's license, how many times did it take you to pass the test?

- What are you the most afraid of on vacation?

- What do you want to get away from the most when you are on vacation?

- What foods smells bad to you?

- What item do you bring on ever trip with you away from home?

- What makes you sleepy?

- What song would you love to hear on the radio when you're cruising on the highway?

- What travel job would you want the least?

- What will you miss most while you are away from home?

- What is something you always wanted to try?

- What is the best road side attraction that you ever saw?

- What is the farthest distance you ever biked?

- What is the farthest distance you ever walked?

- What is the weirdest thing you needed to buy while on vacation?

- What is your favorite candy?

- What is your favorite color car?

- What is your favorite family vacation?

- What is your favorite food?

- What is your favorite gas station drink or food?

- What is your favorite license plate design?

- What is your favorite restaurant?

- What is your favorite smell?

- What is your favorite song?

- What is your favorite sound that nature makes?

- What is your favorite thing to bring home from a vacation?

- What is your favorite vacation with friends?

- What is your favorite way to relax?

- Where is the farthest place you ever traveled in a car?

- Where is the farthest place you ever went North, South, East and West?

- Where is your favorite place in the world?

- Who is your favorite singer?

- Who taught you how to drive?

- Who will you miss the most while you are away?

- Who if the first person you will contact when you get to your destination?

- Who brought you on your first vacation?

- Who likes to travel the most in your life?

- Would you rather be hot or cold?

- Would you rather drive above, below, or at the speed limited?

- Would you rather drive on a highway or a back road?

- Would you rather go on a train or a boat?

- Would you rather go to the beach or the woods?

TRAVEL BUCKET LIST

1.

2.

3.

4.

5.

6.

7.

8.

9.

10.

NOTES

Made in the USA
Columbia, SC
13 January 2023

10206978R00059